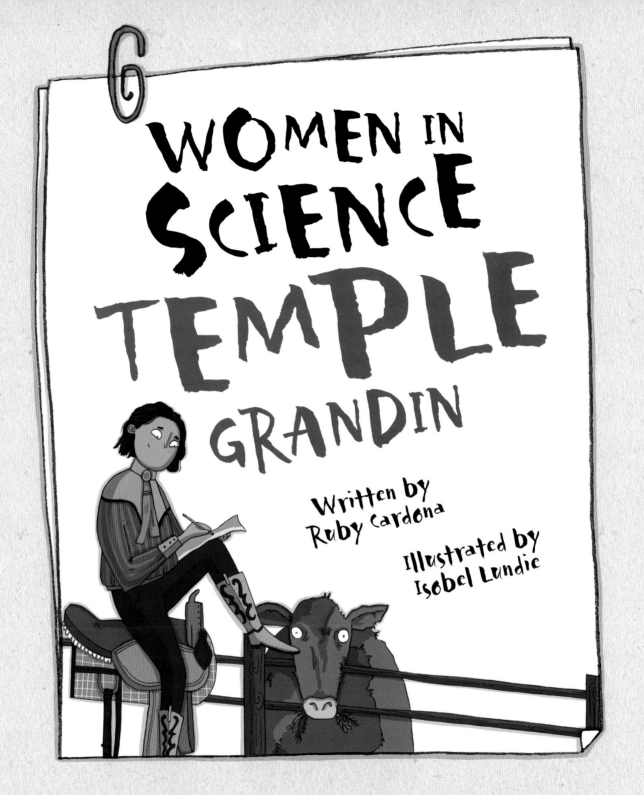

WOMEN IN SCIENCE
TEMPLE GRANDIN

Written by
Ruby Cardona

Illustrated by
Isobel Lundie

Franklin Watts®
An Imprint of Scholastic Inc.

Author:

Ruby Cardona is a history graduate from the University of Bristol in England. She specializes in educational biographies of women.

Artist:

Isobel Lundie graduated from Kingston University in 2015 where she studied illustration and animation. She is interested in how colorful and distinctive artwork can transform stories for children.

Editor:

Nick Pierce

Thanks:

The author and the Salariya Book Company would like to thank Temple Grandin for her involvement in checking the text.

Photo credits:

p.25 dominika zarzycka / Shutterstock.com
p.26 Steve Jurvetson
Shutterstock and Wikimedia Commons.

PAPER FROM
SUSTAINABLE
FORESTS

Published in Great Britain in 2020 by
The Salariya Book Company Ltd
25 Marlborough Place, Brighton BN1 1UB

Library of Congress Cataloging-in-Publication Data

Names: Cardona, Ruby, author. | Lundie, Isobel, illustrator.
Title: Temple Grandin / Ruby Cardona ; illustrated by Isobel Lundie.
Description: New York : Franklin Watts, an imprint of Scholastic Inc., 2020.
 | Series: Women in science | Includes index.
Identifiers: LCCN 2019008970| ISBN 9780531235362 (library binding) | ISBN
 9780531239537 (paperback)
Subjects: LCSH: Grandin, Temple--Juvenile literature. | Animal
 scientists--United States--Biography--Juvenile literature. |
 Autism--Patients--Biography--Juvenile literature.
Classification: LCC SF33.G67 C367 2020 | DDC 636.0092 [B] --dc23

All rights reserved.
Published in 2020 in the United States
by Franklin Watts
An imprint of Scholastic Inc.

Printed and bound in China.
Printed on paper from sustainable sources.
1 2 3 4 5 6 7 8 9 10 R 27 26 25 24 23 22 21 20

CONTENTS PAGE

IMPORTANT PLACES
IN TEMPLE'S LIFE

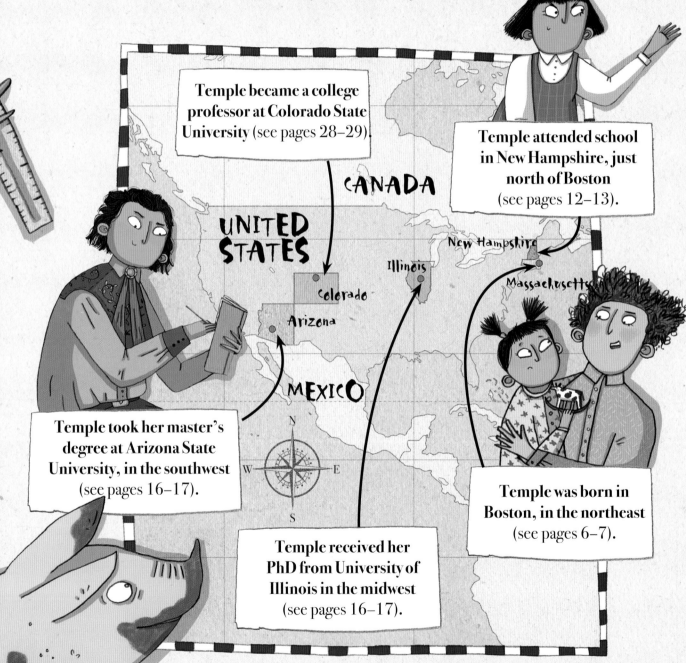

Temple became a college professor at Colorado State University (see pages 28–29).

Temple attended school in New Hampshire, just north of Boston (see pages 12–13).

CANADA

UNITED STATES

New Hampshire

Illinois

Massachusetts

Colorado

Arizona

MEXICO

Temple took her master's degree at Arizona State University, in the southwest (see pages 16–17).

N
W E
S

Temple received her PhD from University of Illinois in the midwest (see pages 16–17).

Temple was born in Boston, in the northeast (see pages 6–7).

INTRODUCTION

Throughout history, there have been many women involved in progressing science and **technology**. Temple Grandin is one of them.

Her inventions in farm technology have changed the way that **livestock** are treated across North America and all over the world. Before, animals were usually treated terribly and often suffered before they died. Thanks to Temple, many of them live far happier lives.

Temple, who has **autism**, has also been a hardworking campaigner for autism awareness. When she was growing up no one knew much about it at all. Today, there is much more understanding of autism and how it can affect people, thanks to the work of people like Temple.

This book tells Temple's story.

A GIRL FROM BOSTON

Mary Temple Grandin was born on August 29, 1947, in Boston, Massachusetts, into a large family. She was the eldest of four children, with two younger sisters and a brother. Although her birth name was Mary, since childhood she was called Temple—her middle name—to avoid confusion with another girl named Mary who worked for the family. The name stuck!

Playing Outdoors

As a child, Temple loved being outside—she spent hours flying her kite, playing in the woods, and building things from scratch. When she was old enough, she spent the summer working on a farm caring for the horses. She fed them and cleaned their stalls.

Boston

Temple

LOOK AT IT GO!

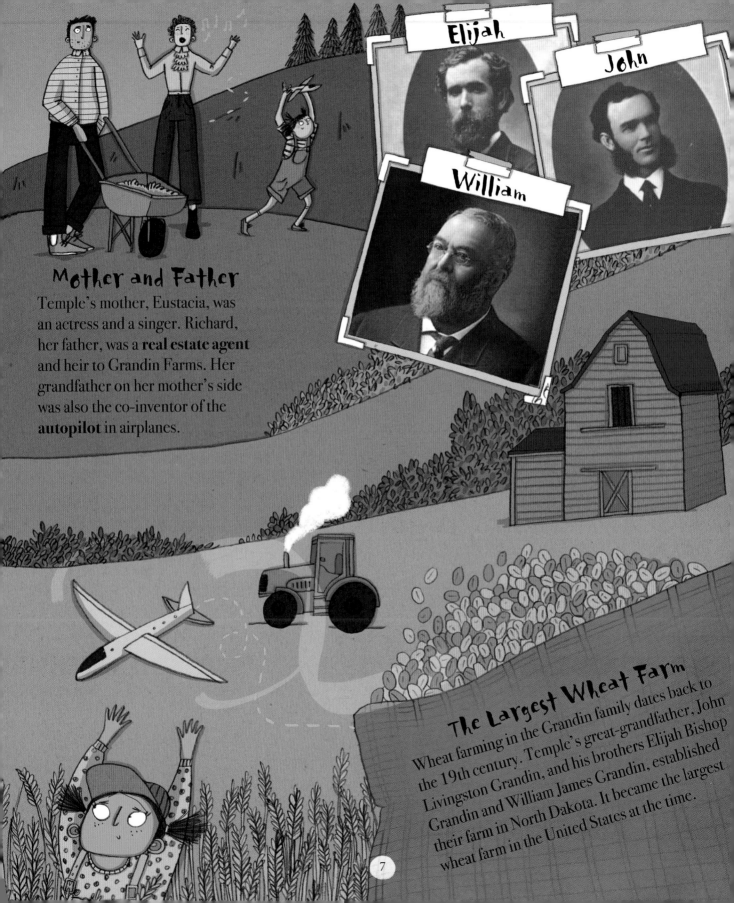

Elijah

John

William

Mother and Father

Temple's mother, Eustacia, was an actress and a singer. Richard, her father, was a **real estate agent** and heir to Grandin Farms. Her grandfather on her mother's side was also the co-inventor of the **autopilot** in airplanes.

The Largest Wheat Farm

Wheat farming in the Grandin family dates back to the 19th century. Temple's great-grandfather, John Livingston Grandin, and his brothers Elijah Bishop Grandin and William James Grandin, established their farm in North Dakota. It became the largest wheat farm in the United States at the time.

A DIFFERENT CHILD

emple's mother could see that her child was different from others: She behaved differently, and had difficulty learning how to talk. But Temple was never **diagnosed** with autism as a child because so little was known about the disorder in those days.

Temple and her mom

I THINK IT MATCHES WITH THIS OBJECT.

Educational Games

At home, Temple had a nanny who played with her for hours each day. She learned important social skills such as waiting and taking turns.

8

Visit To The Doctor

When Temple was a toddler, her mother took her to see a **neurologist**. At the time, lots of doctors recommended that children like Temple be sent away to special homes. But this one recommended she have a **speech therapist**. Temple's family was determined that she should live as normal a life as possible. So Temple was kept at home with her family instead of being sent away.

GOOD JOB.

Signs and Symptoms of Autism

Today we know that autism has many different **symptoms**, and they vary from child to child. Common symptoms of autism in young children can include:

- Finding it hard to learn to talk
- Finding it hard to understand other people talking
- Preferring to play alone rather than with other children
- Feeling uncomfortable about hugging or touching people
- Finding it hard to cope in a group of people

Some kids with autism also have special skills in music, art, math, or visual memory.

WHAT IS AUTISM?

Autism is a disorder that can affect all kinds of people, from brilliant computer programmers to someone who never learns to talk. The disorder usually begins in early childhood. It is a condition that can cause someone to have trouble learning, communicating, and forming relationships with people. Around one-third of people with autism are non-verbal, which means that they do not speak at all.

THIS IS ALL GETTING TOO MUCH FOR ME!

Communication

It is not just talking and listening that those with autism can find difficult. It can be other forms of communication, such as tone of voice or facial expressions, that are hard to understand.

Routine

Those with autism tend to enjoy routine and will repeat certain behaviors, such as choosing to eat the same foods or walking the same routes.

Four Times More Likely

Boys are roughly four times more likely to be diagnosed with autism than girls.

Almost Two Percent

Autism affects almost two percent of people worldwide. In the United States, three-and-a-half million are living with the disorder.

Austism Spectrum

In medicine, some conditions are seen as **spectrums** because they can have many different symptoms and range from being mild to severe. For example, some people find speaking difficult for their entire lives. Others, like Temple, are able to speak as naturally as anyone else once they have been taught.

LIFE AT SCHOOL

School was difficult for Temple. She was **bullied** because of the way she spoke. And since she found communication and speech difficult, this only made it harder. She ended up leaving Beaver Country Day School at fourteen because of conflicts with other children.

Private Boarding School

When Temple was fourteen her mother sent her to Mountain Country School, a **boarding school** in New Hampshire for young people with behavioral problems.

MISS! EVERYONE IS BEING MEAN TO ME!

MISS! IT'S NOT TRUE!

CAN I SHOW YOU MY WORK, SIR?

Finding A Mentor

At her new school, Temple met William Carlock, a science teacher who had previously worked for NASA. This was an important meeting for Temple, and Carlock's teaching had a big impact on her. Later in life, she said that he had focused on her underlying talents and engaged with her on her own terms instead of trying to change her.

KIDS, PLEASE, CALM DOWN!

Holiday Work

During the school holidays, Temple still worked hard— she had a job sewing clothes in her parents' home neighborhood.

Beaver Country Day School

TEMPLE'S HUG BOX

As a teenager, Temple experienced high levels of anxiety as a result of her autism, especially in social situations. Noisy, crowded areas often made her feel tense. But like many people with autism, she found that the feeling of **pressure** was soothing. Since hugging or being touched by other people was uncomfortable, she needed a solution.

Visiting Her Aunt's Ranch

One day, when she was visiting her aunt's **ranch** in Arizona, she saw how squeeze chutes used on the ranch to restrain the cows were highly effective at calming them down.

HMM, I THINK I HAVE AN IDEA...

Notes On Squeeze Chutes

- Usually used for cows
- Apply **compression** without hurting the animal
- Pressure is applied evenly across the body.

Temple's aunt's ranch

Temple's Inspiration

1. The cow steps in...

2. The machine closes around the cow...

3. And pressure is applied.

Temple's hug box

Temple's Invention

Temple had a clever idea to mimic the feeling of being hugged by a person. She called it the hug box. It is made from two large boards of wood which form a "V" shape. The inside is lined with a thick, soft padding. The boards squeeze the person inside. The pressure can be controlled by the box's user. Hug boxes are now used throughout the United States to help autistic adults and children.

A cow being restrained

COLLEGE EDUCATION

After **graduating** from high school, Temple studied for a **psychology** degree at Franklin Pierce College. At college she became interested in animal behavior, particularly that of farm animals such as cows and pigs.

An Accomplished Student

Temple has earned a bachelor's degree, a **master's** degree, and a **PhD**.

HI THERE, FELLA.

Animal Behavior

While studying for her PhD in animal science, Temple became interested in how animals react to their environment. For her **dissertation**, a long piece of scholarly research, she looked at pigs on farms and how their brains develop in response to their surroundings. Temple was also interested in the management and **welfare** of farm animals.

Calm, happy pigs

Human contact

Living in pairs

Hanging cloths

What Pigs Like

Temple discovered that pigs are highly sensitive to their environment. She found that they are calmer and will fight with each other less when they have access to regular contact with other pigs and humans and toys such as hanging cloths.

17

GETTING INTO THE MEAT INDUSTRY

Before Temple became involved in the meat industry, animals bred for meat were usually treated badly. They were generally unhappy, and they suffered before they died. Temple set out to change this.

Farmers

Most of the farmers at the time did not want to change their farming methods.

THIS IS WHERE I KEEP THE LIVESTOCK...

Earning Respect

Temple had to work hard to gain the respect of people in the meat industry. It was made harder by the fact that she was one of the only women doing her job.

Secretaries

Temple remembers that there were very few women working in the **feed yards**, but all the secretaries in the offices would be women.

McDonald's

In the 1990s, Temple found a helpful partner to work with. McDonald's, the giant fast-food chain, took her on as a **consultant** to improve the happiness of their animals. She was able to bring in changes to ensure animals were being well treated.

Crowded Places

Temple has said she feels a deep connection to animals. She has spoken widely about the anxiety she feels in loud, crowded public places, caused by her autism, and how she can feel threatened. This is similar to how animals can feel, especially in scary places such as an **abattoir**, where their lives will come to an end.

Written by Temple Grandin

ANIMALS MAKE US HUMAN

Temple's bestselling book uses her experience of autism to give a unique view on animals—how they think and feel.

What Animals Need

What does an animal need to have a good life? This is what Temple wondered when she wrote her book *Animals Make Us Human*. She explores what is needed for animals' well-being. Some of the things needed include: Access to food, freedom to move around, and freedom from pain or injury. Animals also need the freedom to behave normally as they would in the wild.

IMPROVING THE LIVES OF CATTLE

Temple has devoted much of her research into improving slaughterhouses and the treatment of livestock animals. She has come up with ideas for abattoirs to reduce the stress and anxiety animals feel while they are there.

CATTLE ENTER HERE

30°

curved loading chute

CURVE HIDES WHAT IS AHEAD

curved Loading Chutes

Loading chutes are the corridors that lead cows to the room where they are killed. As Temple discovered from her research, cattle are very aware of their surroundings and can become easily distressed. Her new design for the chute is curved, so the cows cannot see what is in front of them. This stops them from panicking.

Temple made many innovations

Holding device for cattle

ADJUSTABLE SIDE

ENTRANCE CHUTE

RAMP

CONVEYOR

Holding Device

Also designed for beef cattle, Temple's device for holding cows can be adjusted to the size of the animal inside. They are essential for keeping cows still and calm while they are transported for slaughter. Before Temple, these devices were not gentle and often squeezed the cow too tightly.

Scoring System

Temple has developed a scientifically-based scoring system for judging the welfare of animals while they are going through abattoirs. This gives farmers a better understanding of how their animals are feeling and they can adjust their practices to improve the animals' welfare.

Her Own Company

Temple has set up her own company, Grandin Livestock Handling Systems, which designs and produces equipment for farms. Many of her designs for improving animal welfare have been introduced in farms across the United States.

23

GLOBALLY SUCCESSFUL

Temple has made a lasting impact to the way that livestock are treated. Her changes in abattoirs have improved the experience for animals and made these places more **humane**. Temple's inventions in farming technology can be found all around the world. She has helped train workers at over two hundred slaughterhouses globally.

United States
Temple's designs for livestock processing are used across roughly half of all cattle farms in North America.

Mexico
Temple's design of a curved chute system is in place in Mexico.

Australia
In parts of Australia, Temple's holding device for keeping a cow still is used.

Awards

Temple has received many awards for her work, including an award from the World Organization for Animal Health for excellent work improving animal welfare. She was also **elected** to the **American Academy of Arts and Sciences**.

Protesters

Controversy

Many activists continue to argue that the innovations developed so far in the meat industry don't go far enough in combating animal cruelty. Some people think that it's impossible to ever construct a humane abattoir. Temple argues that an ethical meat industry can be achieved if her ideas are built upon.

LOVE ANIMALS

HELP US HELP THEM

ANIMALS ARE NOT OURS TO USE

SHARING HER STORY

While being busy with her career in animal farming, Temple has found the time to campaign for autism awareness. She has been praised for breaking down **stigma** around the disorder and helping people to understand how those with autism think. It is important to her that people have a better understanding.

Temple giving a talk

Public Speaking

Temple has toured the United States making speeches about autism. She is now in high demand to give talks, particularly to audiences who are struggling to understand the disorder, such as the parents of autistic children.

AUTISM ISN'T SOMETHING TO BE AFRAID OF...

Movie Star

Temple's life story made it onto the screen in 2010 when HBO produced a film about her called *Temple Grandin*, starring the actress Claire Danes.

Big Changes

Throughout Temple's lifetime, the public awareness and treatment of people with autism has changed significantly. She has played an important role in bringing change through her speeches, articles, and books.

Books

Temple has written a number of books on autism and her experience of it. At first, she believed that all people with autism think in the same way. Her later works show that she has changed her mind and understands that autistic brains vary greatly. In *The Autistic Brain: Thinking Across the Spectrum* (2013) she writes about the history of autism and explore what it means to be autistic.

Temple Grandin

Temple Grandin

THE AUTISTIC BRAIN

TIMELINE OF TEMPLE'S LIFE

1970

Temple graduates from Franklin Pierce University, New Hampshire, with a degree in psychology.

1947

Temple is born.

1986

Temple writes her first book about autism: *Emergence: Labelled Autistic.*

1963

Temple begins inventing the hug box.

1962

Temple is inspired by science teacher, William Carlock.

1975

Temple completes her Master's degree from Arizona State University in animal science.

1949

Temple is taken to the doctors because of her behavior.

1966

Temple graduates from high school.

1990

Temple becomes a professor of Animal Science at Colorado State University.

1995

Temple publishes another book about how she sees the world: *Thinking in Pictures*.

2010

A film about Temple's life is made, and wins an Emmy.

1989

Temple completes her Animal Science PhD from the University of Illinois.

2009

Temple writes her bestselling book: *Animals Make Us Human*.

2013

Temple writes a new book about autism and her experience with it: *The Autistic Brain: Thinking Across the Spectrum*.

1992

Temple starts working with McDonald's.

GLOSSARY

Abattoir
Place where animals are killed for their meat.

American Academy of Arts and Sciences
An organization dedicated to studying important social, scientific, and intellectual problems. It is one of the oldest groups of its kind in the United States.

Autism
A developmental disorder that starts in childhood which makes it difficult for people to communicate and understand other people.

Autopilot
The system that allows an airplane to fly without a human controlling it.

Boarding school
A school students live in during the semester.

Bullied
When someone is subjected to physical or verbal abuse by someone else who is bigger or has another form of power over them.

Compression
Squeezing something together or into a smaller space.

Consultant
An expert in a certain area who gives advice and guidance to other people.

Diagnosed
When an illness or condition is determined from the symptoms shown.

Dissertation
A long piece of writing on a particular subject, usually written for a college degree.

Elected
When someone is chosen for a job by a system of votes.

Feed yard
The place where livestock animals are fed on large farms. They can feed thousands of animals at a time.

Graduating
To complete high school or college.

Humane
A compassionate or kind way of treating something or someone.

Livestock
Animals kept on a farm, such as cows or pigs.

Master's

Academic study taken after completing an undergraduate degree at a college.

Neurologist

A type of doctor who studies and treats diseases of the nerves and nervous system.

PhD

An advanced degree awarded to people who have done research into a certain topic.

Psychology

The scientific study of the mind and how it influences our behavior.

Pressure

The force or weight of something pressing against something else.

Ranch

A farm in the United States that breeds livestock (animals).

Real estate agent

Someone who deals with buying and selling property. They can help you find a new house.

Spectrum

A wide range of related things, such as medical symptoms.

Speech therapist

A person who helps others learn how to speak more clearly.

Stigma

Negative ideas that people have about particular illnesses or conditions.

Symptom

A change or sign in the body or mind that you are not healthy.

Technology

Using science to invent new machines and other things that can be used in industry.

Welfare

The health and happiness of an animal or human.

INDEX